REVISED AND UPDATED

Transportation Around the World

Cars

Chris Oxlade

Heinemann Library
Chicago, Illinois

Customer Service 888-454-2279
Visit our website at www.heinemannraintree.com

Designed by Kimberly R. Miracle, Ray Hendren, Cavdweller Studio and Q2A Creative
Printed in China by South China Printing Company

12 11 10 09
10 9 8 7 6 5 4 3 2

New edition ISBN-10:   1-4329-0200-8 (hardcover)
                        1-4329-0209-1 (paperback)
New edition ISBN-13:   978-1-4329-0200-1 (hardcover)
                        978-1-4329-0209-4 (paperback)

The Library of Congress has cataloged the first edition as follows:
Oxlade, Chris.
        Cars / Chris Oxlade.
                p. cm. — (Transportation around the world)
        Includes bibliographical references and index.
Summary: Brief text and photographs explain what cars are, describe different types of cars, and examine how they developed and how they are used.
ISBN 1-57572-302-6 (lib.)
1.   Automobiles — Juvenile literature. [1. Automobiles.] I. Title. II. Series.

TL147. 0938 2000
629.2 — dc21
                                                                00-027548

Acknowledgments
The publisher would like to thank the following for permission to reproduce photographs: Alamy p. **4** (Duncan Snow); Allsport pp. **20** (Mark Thompson), **21** (David Taylor), **28** (David Taylor); Auto-express pp. **5** (Dave Smith), **16**, **27** (Dave Smith); Corbis pp. **8** (Bettmann), **12**, **13** (David G. Hauser), **14** (David G. Hauser), **15** (W. Perry Conway); Image Bank p. **19** (L.D. Gordon); Quadrant pp. **9** (Flight), **10** (Felix), **18** (Simon Matthews), **22** (Pete Trafford); The Stock Market pp. **11**, **17**; Tony Stone Images pp. **7** (Christopher Bissell), **21** (Paul Souders), **24** (Simon Bruty), **25** (David Madison); Trip pp. **6** (H. Rogers), **23** (D. Palais), **26** (H. Rogers).

Cover photograph reproduced with permission of Rex Features (Paul Cooper).

Every effort has been made to contact copyright holders of any material reproduced in this book. Any omissions will be rectified in subsequent printings if notice is given to the publisher.

Contents

Some words are shown in bold, **like this**. You can find out what they mean by looking in the glossary.

What Is a Car?

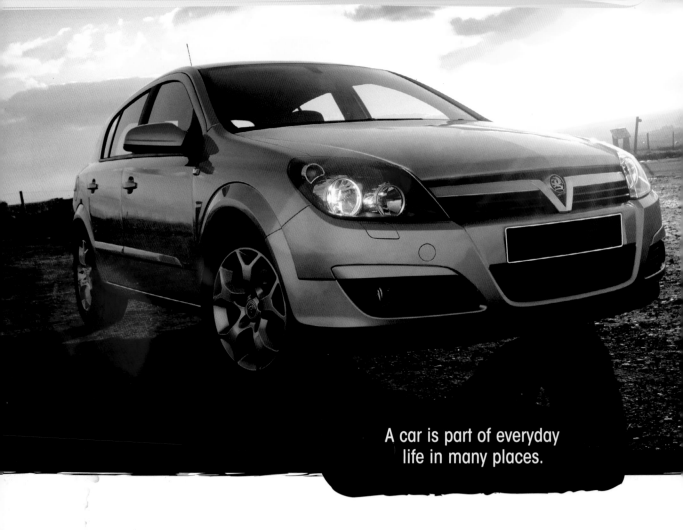

A car is part of everyday life in many places.

A car is a machine that moves along on wheels. Many people use cars to go to school or work every day. Inside a car there are seats for the driver and the passengers.

steering wheel

pedals

Drivers need to know how to use all the controls in a car.

The car goes to the left or right when the driver turns the **steering wheel**. The driver makes the car go faster or slower by using pedals. The pedals are on the floor of the car.

How Cars Work

Most cars have four wheels. Each wheel has a **rubber** tire. The tires roll along the road and stop the car from sliding sideways as it goes around a corner.

Tires need to be changed when they get damaged.

The person who fixes a car is called a **mechanic**.

Every car has an **engine** that makes the wheels turn around. The engine needs **fuel** to make it work. The fuel is stored in a large **tank**.

Old Cars

One of the first cars was made in 1885. It was built by Karl Benz of Germany. It was like a **carriage**, but it had an **engine** instead of a horse to pull it along.

The first cars like this were very noisy and dangerous.

At first, very few people could afford a car. When the Ford Model T was built, it was cheap enough for many people to buy. More than 15 million Model Ts were made.

This Ford Model T had a top speed of 45 miles (72 kilometers) per hour.

R 1878

Classic Cars

Some cars are special because of the way they look. They are called classic cars. Classic cars are often old cars that have been carefully looked after.

This classic Ford Thunderbird was built in the United States in 1956.

Some people collect classic cars. They spend hours polishing all the parts of the car. They display the car at classic car shows.

Many classic cars have shiny trim and fancy lights.

Where Cars Are Used

These cars are traveling in a big city.

Most cars travel along roads. Roads are hard and smooth. Lines are drawn on roads to show drivers the lanes they should drive in.

Cars that drive on dirt roads
are heavy and strong.

In some places there are no paved roads, so cars
travel on dirt roads. Dirt roads are often rough and
bumpy. In the winter, they can become very muddy.

Four-Wheel Drive

In a four-wheel drive car, the **engine** is joined to all four wheels. This makes it easier to drive the car along muddy or icy roads. Four-wheel drive cars can go up very steep hills.

tire

Cars with four-wheel drive have wide tires.

tread

Tread stops the wheels from slipping in mud or ice.

Four-wheel drive cars have tires with a chunky **rubber** pattern, called tread. They have big wheels. The wheels keep the bottom of the car high off the bumpy ground.

Family Cars

SUV is short for *sport utility vehicle*. SUVs often have more seats than other family cars. Big SUVs can be driven on rough, muddy, or icy roads.

SUVs are used in cities as well as in the country.

There is plenty of room for people and shopping bags in a van.

Many family cars need to have a lot of space. Family cars need to have a big trunk. Sometimes the seats in cars fold down to make space for shopping bags, suitcases, or other equipment.

Limousines

A limousine is a very long, fancy car. The person who drives it is called a chauffeur. People hire limousines for special occasions.

A limousine driving down the street always attracts attention.

The seats inside a limousine are big and comfy, like armchairs. Some limousines have a television and a telephone. Some even have a fridge for drinks.

television

A limousine has plenty of space to have meetings or to relax.

Stock Cars

In some countries, stock cars are used for racing around oval **tarmac** tracks. They are allowed to bump and bash into each other. Strong bars protect the driver in case the car rolls over.

Stock cars are made strong so that the driver does not get hurt.

In the United States,
stock cars go very fast.

Stock car racing is very popular in parts of the
United States. The cars race, but they are not
allowed to bump into each other. The driver gets in
the car through a window instead of using the door.

Dragsters

tires

Dragsters have a shape that helps them go very fast.

Dragsters are racing cars that race along a short, straight track. They have huge **engines**. Dragsters have monster tires covered with sticky **rubber**.

parachutes

parachutes

helmet

Dragster drivers wear helmets
to keep them safe.

A drag race lasts for only a few seconds, but the
cars can reach 200 miles (320 kilometers) per hour.
The cars use parachutes to slow down at the end of
the race.

Racing Cars

Car racing takes place on a special track. The cars travel at up to 220 miles (350 kilometers) per hour. Driving a racing car takes a lot of skill.

Car racing is very exciting to watch.

spoiler

Mechanics work quickly so that a pit stop takes only a few seconds.

As the car speeds along, air goes over and under its spoiler. The air presses the car down so that it does not slide around on the track. The car makes a **pit stop** when it needs work on it.

Electric and Hybrid Cars

Some cars have an **electric motor** instead of an **engine. Batteries** inside the cars make the electricity that the motor needs. The batteries need to be recharged when the electricity is used up.

This electric car is small and does not use too much **fuel**. It is just right for city driving.

A hybrid car uses less fuel than a normal gasoline-fueled car.

A hybrid car is a car that uses both gasoline and electricity. It can go as fast and as far as normal gasoline-fueled cars. It does not cause as much **pollution** as other cars.

Jet Power

A car called Thrust SSC was built to go faster than the speed of sound. It can travel faster than 775 miles (1,250 kilometers) per hour. This is as fast as a fighter aircraft can fly.

Thrust SSC was made to go faster than any other vehicle on land.

Thrust SSC has **engines** taken from a jet aircraft.
A jet of hot gases shoots out of the back of the
engines. This pushes the car forward.

Timeline

1885   The first car is built in Germany by Karl Benz. It has three wheels and is driven along by a gasoline **engine**. Its top speed is 8 miles (13 kilometers) per hour.

1894   The first car race starts in Paris, France. The cars race each other to the city of Rouen.

1906   The first luxury Rolls-Royce car is sold. It is built by British engineers Charles Rolls and Henry Royce.

1908   In the United States, the Ford Motor Company builds the first Model T. The company is started by Henry Ford.

1936   The first Volkswagen Beetle is built in Germany.

1996   General Motors builds the first modern electric car that people can buy.

1997   Toyota builds the first hybrid car that people can buy. The Toyota Prius is first sold in Japan, but becomes very popular in the United States by 2003.

2004   BMW unveils the world's fastest car, powered by hydrogen gas. It is called the H2R and can go faster than 185 miles (300 kilometers) per hour.

Glossary

battery   device that stores electricity. The electricity is gradually used up as the battery is used.

carriage   wheeled vehicle usually pulled by a horse

electric motor   machine that powers movement using electricity. Electric cars have electric motors.

engine   machine that powers movement using fuel. A car's engine moves the car along.

fuel   anything that burns to make heat. In a car, the fuel is a liquid called gasoline or diesel oil.

mechanic   person who fixes cars

pit stop   when a racing car stops during a race to get new tires and more fuel

pollution   waste and poisons that go into the air, water, and soil

rubber   soft, flexible material used to make tires for vehicles

steering wheel   wheel inside a car that makes it turn left or right

tank   container in a car where fuel is stored

tarmac   mixture of small stones and sticky tar that makes up the smooth surface of a road

Find Out More

Levinson, Nancy Smiler. *Cars.* New York: Holiday House, 2004.

Raum, Elizabeth. *The History of the Car.* Chicago: Heinemann Library, 2008.

Zemlicka, Shannon. *From Iron to Car.* Minneapolis, MN: Lerner, 2003.

Index